Meet a Baby Rabbit

Jennifer Boothroyd

Lerner Publications • Minneapolis

For the
Sieberer family

Lerner Publications Company
A division of Lerner Publishing Group, Inc.
241 First Avenue North
Minneapolis, MN 55401 USA

For reading levels and more information, look up this title at www.lernerbooks.com.

Library of Congress Cataloging-in-Publication Data

The Cataloging-in-Publication Data for *Meet a Baby Rabbit* is on file at the Library of Congress.
ISBN 978-1-5124-0802-7 (lib. bdg.)
ISBN 978-1-5124-1240-6 (pbk.)
ISBN 978-1-5124-1029-7 (EB pdf)

Manufactured in the United States of America
1 — BP — 7/15/16

Table of Contents

Baby Bunnies 4

Getting Bigger 11

Time to Eat 16

Growing Up 22

Why People Raise Rabbits 28

Fun Facts 29

Glossary 30

Further Reading 31

Index 32

Baby Bunnies

Look at the tiny pink babies lying in a nest. Those little baby rabbits were just born.

Rabbits on a farm live in a hutch. The hutch gives them a safe and clean place to live.

Hutches are made of wood or metal and wire.

The farmer puts a nesting box in the hutch a few days before the baby rabbits are born. The mother rabbit fills the box with straw and some of her own fur. The nest is soft and warm.

This rabbit made a comfortable nest for her babies.

Baby rabbits are called kittens or kits. A group of kits born at the same time is called a litter. Most litters have seven or eight kits.

That's a lot of brothers and sisters!

Kits are born without hair.
They can't see or hear.

These kits depend on their
mother to protect them.

The kits grow quickly. In a week, they are covered in soft fur. Some of the kits are the same color as their mother or father. Some are a different color.

Rabbits can be brown, black, gray, or white. Sometimes they have spots or stripes.

In two weeks, the kits can open their eyes to see. They can also hear with their ears.

Getting Bigger

The farmer removes the nesting box from the hutch. The kits begin to explore their home.

The brothers and sisters play with one another. Playing makes their muscles stronger.

Rabbits often jump into the air and twist around. This move is called a binky.

Baby rabbits sleep a lot during the day and at night. They are more active at dawn and dusk.

When the kits are a month old, the farmer marks their ears. The marks help the farmer tell the rabbits apart.

Time to Eat

A mother rabbit makes milk for the kits to drink. Eight babies can drink at the same time.

The milk is very good for the babies. It contains so many nutrients that the mother feeds the babies only once a day.

Healthy kits have full, round stomachs.

The farmer weans the kits about a month after they are born. They no longer drink milk from their mother.

Most rabbit pellets are made of hay.

The farmer feeds the kits food pellets. These pellets are made especially for rabbits.

Rabbits need to drink fresh
water every day.

Sometimes the farmer
may give the rabbits fresh
carrots or bits of apple.

Rabbits also eat hay,
lettuce, and other plants.

Growing Up

When the farmer weans the rabbits, he puts them into different hutches. The male rabbits are usually in a hutch alone so they don't fight.

Male rabbits are called bucks. Female rabbits are called does.

Rabbits have long feet and strong legs. They can run more than 20 miles (32 kilometers) per hour. They can jump almost 3 feet (1 meter) off the ground.

A rabbit can turn its ears to listen for danger. A rabbit will freeze or hide under something when it is scared. Some stamp their back foot to warn other rabbits of danger.

Rabbits can hear sounds up to 2 miles (3 km) away.

Rabbits are really good at digging. Fences need to be stuck deep into the ground. Otherwise, the rabbits will dig underneath the fence and run away.

Rabbits spend much of their day grooming. They lick their fur clean. To clean its ears, a rabbit will lick its paw and rub its ears.

Grooming helps rabbits stay healthy.

Most of the rabbits will be sold before they are old enough to have babies. Some rabbits will be kept to breed.

A rabbit can have babies when it is six months old.

Why People Raise Rabbits

Rabbits are raised all around the world. Farmers raise rabbits for their meat and fur. People have been eating rabbit meat for thousands of years. Rabbit meat is very healthful. One rabbit can produce 4 pounds (1.8 kilograms) of meat. Rabbit fur is used in clothing. It is also used to make felt or yarn. Rabbits are sometimes kept as pets. Many kids learn about raising livestock by raising rabbits.

Fun Facts

- Angora rabbits have long, soft fur. The fur is cut a few times each year. It can be made into yarn for knitting.

- Rabbits can be trained like a cat or a dog. They can come when called or do tricks. Some can use a litter box like a cat.

- A rabbit's teeth never stop growing. Chewing food and rubbing the teeth together keep them from growing too long.

- Pennsylvania is one of the top rabbit-farming states in the United States.

Glossary

binky: a twisting jump

breed: to produce babies

grooming: cleaning and caring for oneself

hutch: a pen where rabbits live

kit: a baby rabbit

litter: a group of babies born at the same time to the same mother

nutrient: a substance that is needed to grow and live

pellet: a small, round piece of something

wean: to get an animal used to foods besides its mother's milk